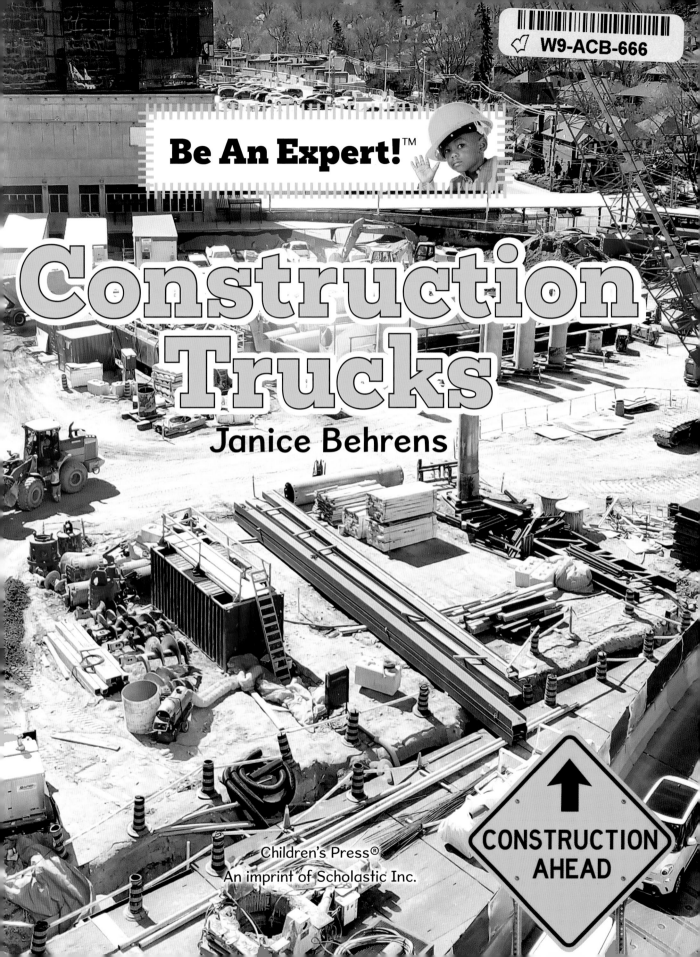

Be An Expert!™

Construction Trucks

Janice Behrens

CONSTRUCTION AHEAD

Children's Press®
An imprint of Scholastic Inc.

Contents

Know the Names

Be an expert! Get to know the names of these BIG machines.

3

Diggers

Here come big diggers!
Dig that dirt.

backhoe

excavator

Bulldozers

Push that dirt.

bulldozer

Zoom In

Find these parts on the bulldozers.

cab **blade** **track** **roller**

bulldozer

Rock Breakers

Break the rocks! Bam!

rock breaker

BAM!

BOOM!

Dig Deeper

Q: What is it like to use a rock breaker?

A: Loud! It bangs like a big hammer. You have to **protect** your ears!

Dump Trucks

Bye-bye, dirt and rocks.

Find these parts on the dump truck.

dump box

cab

wheel

piston

Forklifts

Here come more trucks!
They are strong.

Expert Fact

Forklifts can carry heavy **loads**. Some can carry loads as heavy as three elephants!

Cranes

They are tall.
They go up, up, up!

crawler crane

mobile crane

Zoom In

Find these parts in the picture.

boom **hook** **outrigger**

telescopic crane

Cement Mixers

Here come the mixers!

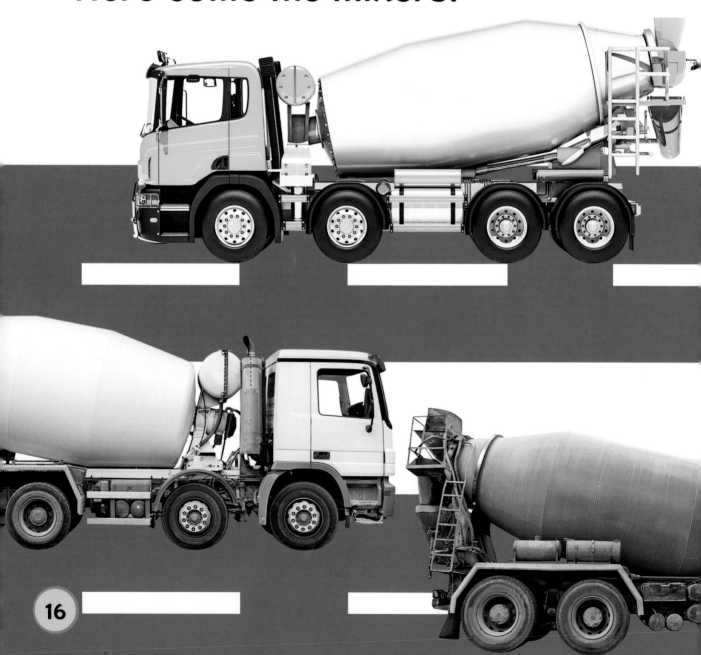

Dig Deeper

Q: Why does the drum keep going around?

A: If it didn't, the cement inside would get hard.

Rollers

Roll out the road!

Big, heavy rollers go slow! They can go slower than a person walking.

All the Trucks

Now the job is done.
Good work, trucks!

1.

2.

5.

6.

Expert Quiz

Do you know the names of these trucks? Then you are an expert! See if someone else can name them too!

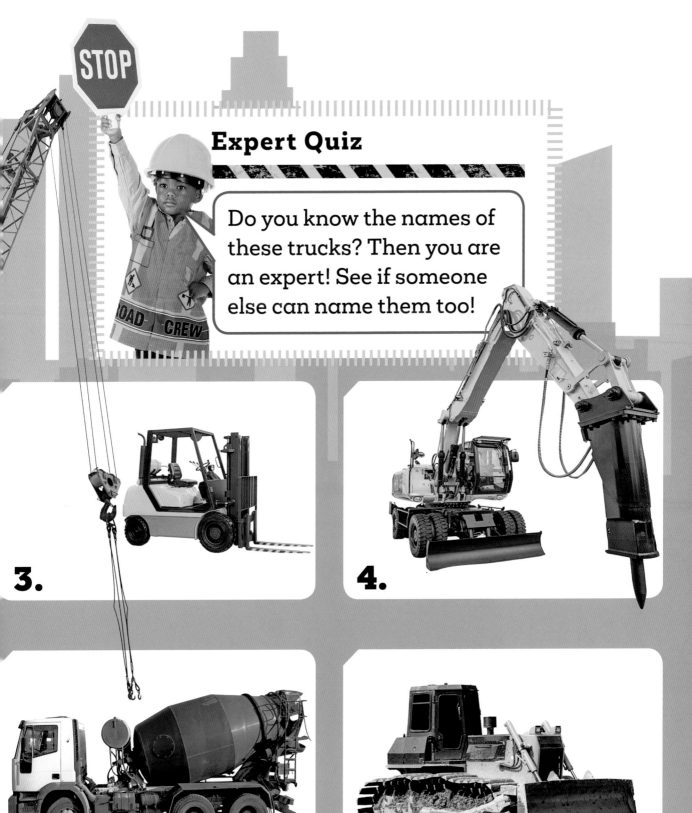

3.

4.

7.

8.

Expert Gear

The worker has cool **gear** to keep safe!

A **hard hat** keeps his head safe.

Goggles keep his eyes safe.

Earmuffs keep his hearing safe.

Gloves keep his hands safe.

Boots keep his feet safe.

Glossary

cab (KAB): where the driver sits in a truck.

gear (GEER): another word for equipment. This is a construction worker's gear.

load (LOHD): something heavy that is carried. The forklift is carrying a load of wood.

protect (pruh-TEKT): to keep safe. The earmuffs protect the worker's ears.

Index

Library of Congress Cataloging-in-Publication Data
Names: Behrens, Janice, 1972- author.
Title: Construction trucks/Janice Behrens.
Description: New York: Children's Press, an imprint of Scholastic Inc. 2020. | Series: Be an expert! | Audience: Grades K-1 | Summary: "Book introduces the reader to construction trucks"—Provided by publisher.
Identifiers: LCCN 2019028540 | ISBN 9780531127643 (library binding) | ISBN 9780531132401 (paperback)
Subjects: LCSH: Construction equipment—Juvenile literature. | Trucks—Juvenile literature.
Classification: LCC TA725 .B44 2020 | DDC 629.225—dc23
LC record available at https://lccn.loc.gov/2019028540

Printed in Heshan, China 62

SCHOLASTIC, CHILDREN'S PRESS, BE AN EXPERT!™, and associated logos are trademarks and/or registered trademarks of Scholastic Inc.

2 3 4 5 6 7 8 9 10 R 29 28 27 26 25 24 23 22 21 20

Scholastic Inc., 557 Broadway, New York, NY 10012.

Art direction and design by THREE DOGS DESIGN LLC.

Photos ©: cover truck: Martin Barraud/Getty Images; cover dirt: carroteater/Shutterstock; cover boy and throughout: glenda/Shutterstock; back cover: Quad Design/Shutterstock; spine and throughout: NirdalArt/Shutterstock; 1 main: NAKphotos/iStockphoto; 1 sign: MicroStockHub/iStockphoto; 2 top left: Anyunoff/Dreamstime; 2 top right and throughout: Ton Bangkeaw/Shutterstock; 2 center right and throughout: mladn61/iStockphoto; 2 bottom left and throughout: glenda/Shutterstock; 2 bottom right and throughout: Lalocracio/iStockphoto; 3 top left and throughout: valio84sl/iStockphoto; 3 top right and throughout: mladn61/iStockphoto; 3 center left: Marko Bukorovic/Dreamstime; 3 center right and throughout: Zts/Dreamstime; 3 bottom right: Thomas-Soellner/iStockphoto; 4 backhoe: Alekcey/Shutterstock; 4-5 city illustration and throughout: Abscent/Shutterstock; 4-5 excavator: RinoCdZ/iStockphoto; 4-5 dirt: motestockphoto/Shutterstock; 5 boy and throughout: Santiago Cornejo/Shutterstock; 6 orange bulldozer: NanoStock/Shutterstock; 6 girl and throughout: Gelpi/Shutterstock; 6 hardhat and throughout: Tommy Studio/Shutterstock; 6-7 bulldozer: Christian Delbert/Dreamstime; 8-9: Salienko Evgenii/Shutterstock; 9 girl and throughout: nicolesy/iStockphoto; 9 woman and throughout: ESB Basic/Shutterstock; 10 dump truck and throughout: Pro-syanov/iStockphoto; 10 road: pingebat/Shutterstock; 11 dirt: vavlt/iStockphoto; 11 dump truck: Zheltobriukh Oleksandr/Shutterstock; 12 forklift: Tricky_Shark/Shutterstock; 12-13 blue forklift: M Carlsson/Shutterstock; 14 crawler crane: VvoeVale/iStockphoto; 14-15 mobile crane: Dragoncello/Dreamstime; 14-15 dirt: Watch The World/Shutterstock; 15 telescopic crane: zorandimzr/iStockphoto; 16 yellow mixer: Pixelci/iStockphoto; 16 white mixer: ollo/iStockphoto; 16-17 red mixer: Konstantinos Moraitis/Dreamstime; 17 man: iodrakon/iStockphoto; 17 striped mixer: Lalocracio/iStockphoto; 18-19: Dmitry Kalinovsky/Shutterstock; 22: John Burke/Getty Images; 23 gear: Moussa81/iStockphoto.